Of Weeping and Wildflowers

Regina M Bergen

Contents

Dedication

This book is for those who have turned
years of struggle into something more—
who rose on weakened steams,
who found a way to grow
despite the weight of the storms.
For the ones who have bloomed,
and for those who are still learning how.
It is for those who have learned
the lessons *Of Weeping and Wildflowers.*

Connections

My problem is that
whenever I manage to
connect with someone
physically, mentally,
or emotionally,
it's never enough.

I want more out of it.
I want to know them,
to really know them.
Surface level isn't
ever going to be able
to satisfy my craving.

I need the deep dive
into who they are,
what they want,
and what molded

them into that
unique individual.

I want the backstory
because without it,
they seem so incomplete
to one who crafts
entire characters out
of nothing but words.

On paper, I can shape
someone into precisely
who I need them to be
through description alone.
In real life, I'm compelled
to seek that information.

I want to understand
the characters in my life
with the same depth I
do my own creations.
But, not everyone wants
to be known on that level.

So, I sit back and
pretend to be content
with whatever morsels
of history I'm provided,
until we grow closer or
I move onto the next story.

Deep Breaths

Just stay busy
to keep the thoughts
of him from your mind.
Deep breaths—in, out.
When the images
sneak in silently at first,
then scream at the
top of their lungs,
it's too late, and
you've waited too long
to find a distraction.
You made it almost
three weeks before
you crumbled this time,
and run back to the
hell you had before.

Manic

There's no mistaking
the rush that takes over,
filling your veins with
purpose and power.
From sad and unable,
to untouchable
(if somewhat unstable)
but still sharp as a tack.
You're torn between
welcoming the pull
with arms wide open
(You know you need it.
You still have dreams.)
or running in fear
from the chaos you
only know how to
incite when your blood
starts to boil with

all the possibilities
of who you could be,
and what you could do
when the dullness
isn't getting in the way,
when you can't sit still
because you're afraid
of missing out on
these moments—
the only times you
still feel like you're alive,
and maybe that's still
worth something.

Tic-Toc

The tic-toc of the clock
is the soundtrack to our
mundane existence now.
The future looms,
ever so ominously,
just above the horizon,
beckoning like the reaper
against the chilly backdrop
of the Doomsday hourglass.
It calls me,
calls the entire free Earth,
to come home as the end
of an era ignites and burns to ashes.
It's the end of the world
as we know it...
But, this time,
not a soul feels fine.

Player Two

I live and breathe in the
empty spaces I've built
from the ground up,
with branches crafted from
the false hope that grew
from my belief in your lies
and trust in your deceptions.
A thousand times over
I fell hard for your words,
so seemingly sweet,
never once questioning
whether they were real
or only a game to you.
And for that, I pay sorely.
A sore loser, I suppose.
Play stupid games, they say,
and you win stupid prizes.
Even if you never knew

your lover was your opponent
until the final round had ended,
leaving you defeated,
choking and gasping for breath.

Situationships

He can't be the one that got away
if he is still the one that never even was.
I fell in love with someone who
didn't exist outside of my heart;
and for that, I suffer in silence.
Because as far as the rest of his
world knows, I was never in it at all.
Love cannot be lost if it was never
found in the first place.

Not Quite Sister Wives

I'm often asked how
I can be so accepting
and even welcoming,
of my former spouse,
his lover, their child,
and, of course, their dog,
after our marital demise.

The truth lies in how
we've come to understand
and accept the reality of
our beginning and ending,
and their inevitability.

Our tale was born of two
lonely young people
searching for love in
all the wrong places

at the right time.

The end came far later
than it should have.
Still, I have no regrets.

When I tuck my children in,
I'm thankful for the events
that brought them into
this world as blessings.

In hindsight, I'm grateful for
our epic crash and burn,
our unraveling,
which granted us the freedom
we so desperately needed
to become who we really are.

The end happened in such
a painful, messy whirlwind.
If you were there, you know.
(But, if you were there,
you'll never truly 'get' it at all)
How we moved past it all and arrived
at this place of friendship.

But, time does heal our wounds.

I firmly believe that
everyone should have
their own true love story-
but I wasn't his, just as he
wasn't ever really mine.

We both welcomed what
came easily to us when
we were young and lonely,
swept out into a sea of:
maybe's, could be's,
and the lure of possibilities.

Those white picket fence dreams
hit hard in your mid-twenties.

It all had to end, though.
If I begrudged someone the
chance to find love, a touch of
magic in an often cruel world,
then all the words I've ever
spouted about kindness,
forgiveness, and compassion

were merely a waste of breath.

Instead, I choose to love
whoever loves me back,
in whatever way that may be,
recognizing that it can change over time,
taking on new, sometimes better,
forms for everyone involved...

It takes a village,
and now, we all finally have one.

Hope

What's that tingle I feel?
It's so little, almost unnoticeable,
a tiny spark of light amidst the dark.
Not a promise by any means,
merely the slightest possibility
that good things may still loom
upon a horizon that, as of late,
only harbored gloom and doom.

The Test

I started seeing someone else.
Last night held a touch of the
magic I've missed since we
began our long, toxic tango.
I had to force myself to open up
to the prospect of new possibilities,
since I still think of you every day.

The irony is, I'd gone out with him before,
then left without a trace
when you waltzed back into my life
for the hundredth time
(at least it feels like that many.)

Somehow, he came back again.
He is legitimately wonderful
(and everything that you're not.)
Sweet, kind, loyal, open, and honest.

I'm not his dirty little secret
to be kept behind closed doors.

In fact, the only problem with him
is, quite simply, that he isn't you...
but no one ever will be, you know.
I swear, the universe is testing me
to see if I'm worthy of someone
better in nearly every way...

Am I fit to receive this man's love?
Will I even let it get close to that?

It's as if you know I'm moving on.
Or did I just manifest you missing me
so you'd know, even for a moment,
the gravity of how it feels to
want what you'll never have?

You reached out before me last night,
for the first time in our long history
of cycling on and off again
(but never really on, though...
always something in between.)

It wasn't as hard as I thought it'd be
to turn off my phone and ignore you.

Maybe all of this time, all I needed
was the closure that came with
knowing you still think of me
every so often, once in a while.

That it was at least a little bit real,
and not in my head all this time.

I won't let myself fall into you again,
throwing away the possibility of
finding something that I've searched
for since the first time we came
together, then tore ourselves apart.

I deserve so much more than a drunk
2 am text because you finally feel
a brief moment of missing me...
This thing between us is finally finished.

Backward Progression

Take me back to the days we were
out until the streetlights blazed on—
cutting into the evening to usher us home
to bedtime snacks and stories of
once-upon-a-time and happily-ever-after.

To crying silly, bleary-eyed tears over
the boys who never really hurt us…
not the way they do now, anyway.

Take me back to the time when friends
were only ever a phone call away,
and never too wrapped up in the
chaos of their day-to-day to pick up.

Take me back to the long drives to see
holiday lights illuminating the darkness,
providing comfort through even the

coldest of the long winter nights.

Take me back to fireflies on a summer eve,
and games of tag in open fields.
To birch beer from the tap at the firehouse
after a softball victory by dad's team,
or getting "lost" on the trails you knew
by heart and mind, then and even now.

Give me those precious days long gone,
free from worry over what new trauma
the next day, week, month, or even year
could be carrying in its wake.

But, even more importantly,
if I can't have it back, can we try to
give it to our children today, at least?

To restore their innocence,
to free those little souls who shouldn't have
to be so strong or resilient just yet,
allowing them to simply exist?

Their burdens are already too heavy,
and they have already seen too much.

I wish I could unsee and unknow some
of the things I learned too soon—
but it's already too late for me.

The Perfect Crime

Like a thief in the night,
you stalked without prejudice,
sneaking in to take what
was still rightfully mine.

You robbed me of years with:
A mother.
A guardian.
A best friend.
A hero.

You lurked in hidden cavities,
shrouded in secrecy,
a criminal housed in a host body
that offered too little evidence on the
outside of a silent battle waged within.

You waited, stealthy, calculating

until it was too late—stage IV—
plotting your takedown in waves.
Like a cunning criminal, well-armed,
you played tricks on our hearts.

You staged your attack from
within the confines of your hideout
while we threw around words like:
Surgery,
Treatment,
Recovery,
Remission,
Recurrence.

Complicated terms that did nothing
to ease her pain or ours.
Then, you repeated the steps,
learning new tricks to give false hope:
"experimental procedures"
and
"clinical trials,"
only to tear that hope away with gloved hands
and long-winded medical terminology.

It was the perfect crime.

No one to blame but chance, right?
At long last... murder in the first degree.
And the only comfort now is
that she's no longer in any pain,
but we are... and you've merely moved
on to identify your next victim.

You took my mother from me,
but you'll never rob me of the memories.

Without You

Sometimes,

without you,

the air is

too thin

to breathe.

It was

the same

when you

were here,

but the wind

carried your

scent in

its wake,

and I survived

on that alone.

Interlude

When you've listened to
a thousand songs together,
it's hard to escape the
memories that come in
waves and flashbacks with
the beat of each melody.
The radio is an instrument
of war against my heart,
striking with callous disregard
over which parts of me survive
and which become casualties
of the war between us.

You

"Are you seeing anyone?" he asked.

"Yeah... but, he's not you," I replied.

It was all I could think to say.

The truth of the matter, its heart,

is that no one will ever be you again.

No one else will ever get me in that way.

I let you overpower me, taking over,

and you still harness that strength.

I grow weak in your presence even now,

but, I've learned a tough lesson:

You can turn my nervous system into

a tornado and leave me reeling.

Then, with carefully chosen words,

you never cease to leave me behind—

lovestruck, heartsick, irreparably broken,

trying to pick up the pieces of myself.

No one else makes hurting feel
so much like true love,
an illusion that leaves me
grappling, wondering, again and again:
What the hell happened while I was
supposed to be safe in your care?

And, still, I want for your words
and, even more, your touch.
Still, I'd be yours in a moment
if you decided that's what you wanted.

I tell someone new he has my heart because
he will give it a better home than
you ever have, or would, or even could...
but you will always live deep within me,
echoing in the hallways of my heart,
a reminder not to let him get too close.

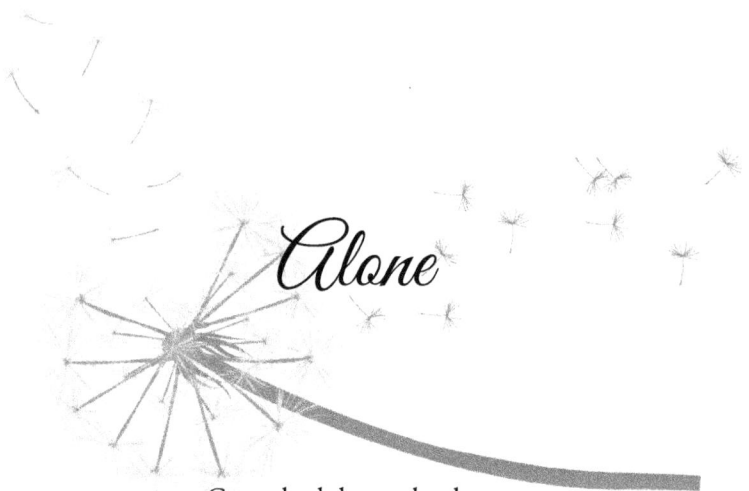

Alone

Crouched down, broken,
on the bathroom floor,
like a shard of porcelain
from the vase that once
held the flowers you brought.

I'm damaged goods now,
an afterthought too far gone
to be pieced back together
in any real sense of the word.

Shattered beyond recognition,
I'm a distant memory of the girl
I had been before you.
And I'm done setting myself ablaze
just to sparkle in your skies.

Flutter

The tragedy of all that we aren't
is that you still incite the flutter of
a thousand tiny butterfly wings
through my nervous system
with just a few sweet nothings
and a glance in my direction.

Your words are a drug.
I'm left breathless, stuttering,
and wondering how I will
walk away from you again
when it becomes obvious that
we are nothing more than
we ever were before...

That this is just the moment
when we reach that familiar point
in our endless cycle where

I start to lose my heart,
knowing, all the while, that
the butterflies always fly away.

Something Like Love

Against the sea of your eyes,
blue-grey with flecks of desire,
I once thought I recognized a faint
glimpse of love or something like it.
Fleeting and timid, but I swore
it was there, just the same.

I mistook your wildness
and passion for possibility...
but you'll never be tamed.
Nor would I aim to break
such a beautiful soul with only
my introspective nature
to act as a companion.

You, who longs only for freedom,
to be unchained from any tethers,
deserve more than you'd ever find

in a greedy heart that clings as tightly
to the love of others as mine does.

I'd be a weight dragging you down
every time you spread your wings,
each time you tried to fly free.
For my place is here on the ground,
while you belong with the stars.

You are light and sound waves,
space dust and cosmic chaos.
I'm flowers and dirt against a
backdrop of books and boredom,
and I no longer have it in me
to pass the long, cold nights
struggling just to illuminate your skies.

It's time to start a new chapter.
There is no happily ever after.
This time, when the story ends,
the girl doesn't get the boy.

It's in the Leaving

How did I know it was truly over?
That the cycle had run its course,
never to repeat like so many times before?
It was in the leaving.
This time, I left without saying goodbye.

Finally, after years wasted
spinning my wheels,
stuck on the carousel of us,
watching familiar scenery
blur past in endless loops,
I turned and walked away.

Not a word, not a sound.
No backward glance
in your direction
to make me
change my

mind.

Just the weight lifting

from my shoulders

with each step.

Deliberate.

Further

away.

Finally free.

Written in the Scars

The wounds that bleed inside
carve valleys deeper than
any blade against skin.
Both inscribe their stories:
the visible, a moment's pain;
the hidden, a lifetime's echo.

A flesh wound mends with time,
threads itself whole again,
while a heart, once broken,
beats to a different rhythm—
forever carrying the weight
of what it lost and learned.

Beneath the Surface

Some scars are visible—
white lines mapping survival
across the landscape of skin,
while others remain unseen,
etched in memory and breath.
Both whisper their truths.
Each carries its purpose.
But while flesh remembers,
then forgives and heals,
the heart holds its wounds
like pressed wildflowers
between the pages of a book—
preserved in perfect detail,
but never quite the same.

Constellations in Your Eyes

Your eyes are glittering stars,
illuminated by the shimmer
of space dust as they
catch the light just right.

When your gaze falls upon me,
it traces my heart in constellations
that lead me, starstruck, to you—
like a star map guiding me to
the ecstasy of your arms.

You've remained a mystery to me,
but it's all part of your allure.
You are faded pages unturned,
a brilliant story still unread.

You are space, vast and unexplored,
a black hole of the unknown.

You, who have confessed to being
an enigma even to yourself.

You say you want depth but pull away,
like me, when things get too real,
when our possibilities become more
than secrets shrouded by fearful tongues.

(Our tongues were always better
at kissing than talking, anyhow.)
Somehow, in the few words spoken,
we always triggered our downfall.

You've never lied to me about
what you were looking for.
I merely turned a cheek,
pretending I could change you.

I believed if I willed it so,
or waited long enough,
you would emerge from behind your walls,
or open the gates into Heaven.

That, finally, you would see the
sheer power that exists in us together,

that you'd feel the fire I'd known since
the moment of our first touch.

All this time, I hopelessly wished
on shooting stars and satellites—
transient, passing in the dead of night,
and leaving no trace behind—
that you'd realize our magic is real.

I should have been learning to love myself,
instead of waiting for you to love me.

Mom

I'm lying in my mama's room,
in my mother's bed.
It's been four long years
that she's been dead.

I'm trying, no, begging to feel
the things I never felt,
but it seems my heart
still isn't ready to admit
she's gone and to
accept that the loss exists.

It's as if she's on vacation,
and I'm house sitting here,
occupying all her spaces,
just waiting for it all
to have been a dream.

Enough

All I ever wanted was for
someone to tell me that
I was enough...
Whether I won the game,
aced the test,
got the lead role,
pulled a 4.0 GPA,
or simply let go
and left it all behind...
All I needed to know
was that it was enough.
That I was enough.
No matter what.
I would have given
my whole world just to
hear you say:
Win,
lose,

or fade away,
we love you just the same.

Safe Space

Today, I was asked whether
I have a "safe place" in my head.
"A what?" I asked, unsure.
"A place where you go in your mind
to feel safe, secure, and protected."

And, honestly, I'd never really
put any thought into it...
And the sad truth is that
the only place I could really
come up with was my first
long-term boyfriend's bed.
The one in his parents' house.

The weirdness doesn't escape me.
But, you see, he saved me from myself,
and for the first time in many years,
he made me feel like I was enough...

His family welcomed me when
it felt like my own was crumbling
all around me, just like everything else.

But, in that room, with the door closed,
air conditioner on, tucked beneath
soft sheets and warm blankets,
enveloped by the first person
to know the deepest parts of me,
I was all of those things:
safe, secure, and protected.
Even more... I was loved.

We were first-time lovers hiding
from a world that didn't understand.
We were an age gap romance
that my parents were wary of,
struggling to prove ourselves.
We were each other's peace.

We were long nights spent cuddling,
and mornings sleeping late.
We were holidays waking together,
even when it made my family mad.
We clung tightly for a long time,

considering our inexperience
(or maybe because of it.)

Decades later, in my forties,
I guess it remains the only
real "safe place" I can conjure
in this anxious mind that, now,
never lets its guard down enough to trust.

You

I loved you once, twice,

then several times more...

Again and again I've tried,

but I still haven't set fire to that cord

that tethers me to you

for all the wrong reasons.

You, who speaks in riddles.

You, who holds me without chains.

You are late-night chats

with a depth that enthralls,

and periods of lengthy silence

in the gaps between calls.

You're all the right buttons,

followed by all the wrong.

You, who I follow like a star.

You, who keeps me at arm's length.

You are yes when I should say no,
my downfall and my strength
when I know I can't manage
the weight of the world
without you as a crutch—
without begging for your pretty words.

You, who I've left behind so many times.
You, who never seem to care
whether I'm gone or whether I'm there.

Dopamine Detox

Step back.

Move!

Give me the space

to come alive,

to find my spark,

to step out from

the cold, the sad, the dark.

Watch my flicker

become an open flame.

Today, I'm winning

the battle against myself.

Today, I'm finding

the strength to be me

without reaching for you.

This time is different

from those that came before.
My head and my heart
stand together as allies,
forces to be reckoned with
as they wage this ongoing war
with a newly-united front.

We are stronger now together
than we ever were apart.

Today, I'm everything
you thought I'd never be.
Today, I'm something new,
burning bigger and brighter than
you ever believed possible.

I cast you into shadows,
left your memory to smolder.
Now, I am white hot fury,
scorching our memories
in a battle to the death,
reducing them to ash in
an inescapable firefight.

This is where we end.

This is how 'us' dies.
Not quietly in a puff of smoke,
but in a blinding inferno,
suffocating our past,
leaving it unrecognizable.

Today, I am all the things that
you never thought I could be.

Today, I'm your nemesis,
born of all the things you'd
never allow us to become.
Now, I see you for what you are:
A toxic, flaming cocktail of
dopamine hits and what if's.

Domestic Cacophony

I'm trying to act
like it doesn't drive
me past an invisible
threshold that lies
somewhere between
normal and insanity
when the kids are
climbing my limbs,
as the dogs walk over me,
digging claws into flesh.

The TV spews some
obnoxious brain rot,
and someone's tablet
or game dings incessantly.
A hint of the need for a
diaper-change wafts by...
Just another need to meet,

something else that can't
wait for a calmer time.

Sometimes it feels like
the house is a war-zone.
I flinch whenever there's
a sudden movement,
as if my life is at risk
merely by sharing the
same space with my
rapidly growing anxiety!

I'm becoming unhinged,
AND MY BRAIN FEELS LIKE
MASHED POTATOES!

Clash

You don't have to shout to be strong
(or to prove you're right).
If you can't convince the storm to soften,
you can still close your windows,
and make your own light.
Then, hold your children in the calm,
safe, protected, loved, and supported
with positivity and forgiveness.
There is a grace in standing still
when others throw their weight in words.
There is a power in not shrinking
even as your tears fall freely
(eternally awful at dry eyes in conflict)
You are not lazy.
You are not less.
You are the light that stays on,
even when no one says thank you.
You strive for peace, for chosen battles.

Let them misjudge you.

Let them mistake your softness for surrender.

You know the truth:

what you carry is heavier than they will ever understand...

and still, you aim to offer warmth,

failing at times, but always a work in progress.

Tonight, let the moon keep your secrets.

Let the silence speak words of comfort:

"I see you. You're still here. You're still good."

And tomorrow, even weary, even cracked,

you will rise like the mother you are.

One who reads emotional cues,

adapts to each child's needs,

and creates a safe space for trust,

free of harshness, free of fear.

A mom not perfect.

But still whole.

Word Magic

Poetry is pure alchemy.
When writing, you harness
a deep magic with no rules.
No limits on form or function,
on heart or healing.
It transmutes confusion into clarity,
shapes pain into art,
and writes silence into language.

Every poem is a way of screaming
into a void that never answered—
So, you answered yourself.

You've written the longing,
the ache that has no name,
even when no one was listening.
Maybe now it's time to write
the escape, the exit, the end of us.

The part where you move on,
writing yourself whole
from the scattered pieces
left behind after enduring
the beauty of the breakdown.

Possibility

The air feels different today—
a hush, a tremble—
like the universe inhaling hope.
There's a subtle shift in the atmosphere,
stirring faint whispers that tomorrow
might hold something more.
Something better.
A shimmer of possibility,
a glimmer of promise after a
long trail of disappointment.
I let the hope carry me, lift my spirits.
But I am wary of false prophets...
Still, I chide myself for the smile
that crosses the contours of my face
when I see his name on my phone.
Don't let your walls come down.
Don't make it easy for him.
What rises fast is sure to fall.

Odds are, he is the next one
in a long line of maybe's, could-be's,
and almost-were's.
Keep your guard up.
Be wary: a possibility
isn't a probability,
and not every maybe is meant
to become more.
No matter how much you want it,
or how long it's been
since you've felt something real.

Slow Down

Whoa, whoa, whoa!

Slow down, girl.

Pump the brakes,

and take five steps back.

You're moving too fast.

You've let the possibilities

overpower the reality.

You don't really know him—

not yet.

You've made this mistake before

and swore you wouldn't do it again.

Wipe the smile off your face

when his name appears

with a flash across your screen.

The buzz of the phone

matches the buzz

in your nervous system

as things go too far, too fast,

and you're left trying

to backpedal

to the place you were before—

untouched,

unhooked,

unharmed.

So pause.

Let the silence stretch.

Breathe between the pings.

Ask the questions

you're scared to know the answers to.

Not everything tender is true.

Not every spark means fire.

You are worth more

than just another

lesson in restraint.

Stay soft,

but stay smart.

Want, but wait.

Let him earn the parts of you

that ache to be seen.

Slow down, girl.

You're not in a race—

you're building a life.

Rush or Run

It starts like music—
easy, electric,
like your skin already knows
what your brain hasn't caught up to.
He laughs,
you answer too quickly.
You text too much,
say too much,
feel too much,
far too fast.
And you know it.
But it feels so good
to be wanted,
to be seen,
to be chosen—even just for now.
You want to believe
this time is different,
that it's okay to lean in

without the usual guardrails.
But even as you reach,
a second self
tightens her grip on the brake.
He touches your hand
and something inside you
shouts run.
Not because it's bad—
because it might be good.
Because if you stay,
he'll see you.
The real you.
And what if that's
too much
or not enough?
You say you want love
but the moment it inches closer,
you lace up your shoes,
eyes on the door.
How can anyone hold you
if your instinct is
to flee the feeling
before it can even prove
you weren't safe in it?
So here you are again,

spinning between
the freefall and the firewall,
half heart on fire,
half foot out the door—
trying to decide
if you'll finally stay
long enough
to find out
what it could become.

Stained Glass

I liked him, I did.
But it all got to be too much
for someone who is used to
never being enough.
The pull toward self-sabotage is strong—
a reflex, a scar-taught dance,
the tendency to implode things
before they get too real,
before they have the chance to
constrict,
to constrain,
to crush
my heart into stained glass shards—
still lovely, but broken just the same.
So I ghosted the good.
I panicked at the kindness.
I mistook comfort for a trap
and tenderness for danger.

I ran.

Not because he hurt me—

but because he didn't.

And I'm still learning

that love doesn't have to come

with sirens,

or smoke,

or pain.

That maybe,

just maybe,

I'm allowed to stay

when things feel right.

Brimstone

We struck a match with words,

and suddenly they became sparks.

Then—

we were on fire.

Fast.

Hot.

Hungry.

Like we'd waited lifetimes

to converge like this.

But somewhere in the burn,

I panicked.

Transformed.

Turned wildfire to brimstone—

all smoke, no breath.

Dead before it even lived.

Ashes where something new

was just beginning to bloom.

I don't know if it was

too far, too fast,
or too right, too soon.
But it started to feel
like a trap
I had built myself.
Like the wish I made
was wrapping its hands
around my throat,
Choking.
Suffocating.
And behind me—
ghosts of almost,
used-to-be,
and what-if—
stood watching.
What if loving you
meant leaving them
behind for good?
No back door left open.
No familiar ache
to curl up in
when this one shatters too.
So I ran—
not because it was wrong,
but because I couldn't bear

how it might be right,
or how much I'd lose
just by choosing you.
We were two stars colliding,
and all that's left
is space dust.

When It Feels Like Too Much

I wanted something real,
but forgot how real can shake you...
how it knocks not with roses
but with overfull inboxes
and someone who doesn't run.
I asked for slow.
Asked for depth.
Asked for someone who'd stay.
But when it came wrapped in
good morning texts
and open-hearted paragraphs,
I nearly sprinted the other way.
I've known hunger.
I've known craving.
I've known the soft ache
of someone half-there,
and called it almost-love.

But now?

Now someone shows up.

And instead of peace,

I feel pressure.

Instead of joy,

I feel trapped.

Because what if this is the thing

that finally asks me

to go all in?

What if I'm too tired to bloom?

What if I open up, and it doesn't last?

What if I build hope again

only to watch it shatter softer this time?

Still—I don't walk away.

Not yet.

I hold the line,

the quiet boundary

between don't leave

and don't rush.

Let me find myself here,

in the still space between

panic and possibility.

Let me remember

that wanting love

doesn't mean I have to drown in it

just to prove I can swim.
I'm learning to trust slow.
To stay curious.
To wait for the part of me
that says:
This feels like safety—finally.

Conditions

I've learned

that attraction comes with conditions.

Flirtation with footnotes.

Touch, with terms...

Often terms I never agreed to.

Desire exists in full bloom,

as long as I stay soft and silent.

Available, but never asking too much.

So I test the waters to see if he runs—

not because I'm cruel,

but because I'm tired of being discarded.

I want someone who stays

when the answer is not yet.

Who wants my laugh

as much as my curves,

my chaos

as much as my calm.

I say, "I want to wait,"

and watch the air shift,
wondering if this is the moment
that I stop being enough this time.
But here's the thing:
I am enough.
Even when I tremble.
Even when I second-guess,
spin out,
and stitch myself back
together with apologies.
If you want me,
you must want the whole of me.
Not just the warmth of my skin,
but the weight of my honesty.
Because love, real love,
should never hinge
on how quickly I choose to
keep or give myself away.

Not Missing Anything

I'm tired of feeling like I'm
still waiting to be finished.
Incomplete, like a draft
begun in earnest,
but never quite completed.

No happy endings here.

I've handed myself over
in outlines and shades of gray,
soft-spoken,
half-hearted,
hoping someone else
might color in the rest.

But I'm not a wound
waiting for stitches.
Not a light that only shines

when someone flips the switch.

I am breath,
and bone,
and laughter,
and rage.

I am sadness born of trauma,
and strength grown in its wake.
Grit beneath my fingernails,
sunlight on the backs of my shoulders.

I am whole.
I am enough.

Even when I second-guess.
Even when I crave elusive arms
that don't tighten, then leave.
Even when the mirror
reflects the scars of the past,
over the woman I am today.

Let them call me too much.
Let them misunderstand the way
my mind churns in overthinking.

I am not missing anything.

I was just never meant

to be finished by someone else.

Even Now

Lately, it feels like the sky is breaking.
The clouds are tired of holding back,
so they shed their tears freely.
The floods come fast,
and fires overtake the places
we once called home,
burning our past into ash,
and submerging our peace.

The earth shifts,
and so do we—
unsteady, unsure,
grieving things we can't quite name.
Headlines blur into the thunder,
dragging our tired, grieving hearts
through the muddy waters.

The ground beneath our feet

doesn't feel secure anymore.

But even now,
in these tiny moments—
the calm after the storm—
a child laughs at the simple joy
of jumping in a muddy puddle.
Light breaks through ash-grey clouds,
and a neighbor knocks,
stopping by just to say:
I'm here to check on you today.

Even now—
on a blanket in the sun,
making its appearance to prove
it still has the power to warm,
a dog curls into the space
where your knees bend,
and you catch a breeze
that smells like honeysuckle—
an aroma reminiscent of childhood,
and an innocence lost to time.
You cry, and someone stays.

The world may tremble,

but somewhere,

a seed pushes upward.

Somewhere,

a heart still chooses kindness

over collapse.

And that is not nothing...

That is how we begin again.

Always the Climb

Some people walk flat roads,
with gentle ebbs and flows,
slight dips between hardship and ease,
slow transitions between traumas.
I don't begrudge them that.
But I was raised on on a hill,
each morning a summit,
each night a slow slide down.

At the earliest glimpse of teenhood,
when my world shifted on its axis,
I grew tired of trying.
Tired of shrinking inside to be accepted,
while wanting to disappear on the outside,
right down to skin and bones... thin is in.
Tired of asking the mirror for
permission to simply be me.
Tired of scales that tipped

too far in the wrong direction.

I became weary of all I saw before me,
bored with the possibilities presented,
overwhelmed with pretenses:
fake smiles and faux friends.
By the time I reached high school,
I learned how to disappear,
to fade away without ever leaving.
I hid in my room, alone.
Lost too soon to those who had
stopped caring about my weekend plans.

I drank too much,
bled in secret,
loved in silence.
I let go of the things I loved
before they could let go of me...
just like the others that came before.

Everyone claimed self-imposed solitude,
but the truth is: I had no choice.
I couldn't face the ones who
weren't like me, who didn't understand.
I envied the girls who didn't

carry powerful storms in their ribs,
who didn't measure their worth in calories,
perceived glances, or silence at dinner.

My life was full of love...
but a love with sharp edges,
resentment grown like ivy
over things we couldn't say out loud.
Secrets pressed on like wallpaper,
then painted over in whitewash.
Betrayals unspoken, hidden from view,
but known by all parties as we
learned the meaning behind
'staying together for the kids.'

These days, I'm stronger.
My walls are higher now,
my floodgates spill-proof.
I've come far.
A spine made of steel,
fashioned from splinters,
and held together with stubbornness.
I know myself now—
but sometimes the knowing
only makes the weight heavier.

I see every pattern
before I fall into it
and still—
sometimes I fall.

I want peace.
But I'm always bracing
for the next steep stretch.
For the next ache I'll have to name
before it names me.

Still I go.
Step by step.
Continuously healing,
but never quite healed.
Always the climb.
Always mine.

Peace Over Pieces

2 a.m.

and the ghosts don't knock—

they slip in.

Soft, like breath.

Like memory.

Like his eyes.

I stare at the ceiling,

wide-awake in a war

between heart and mind.

Both traitors.

Both whispering,

"Maybe this time, it'll feel like it used to."

My thumb hovers

over his phone number—

trembling like it knows

what it cost me to walk away.

To stay away.

And still,

some cruel part of me

misses the warmth

of something

that never even existed.

Just the way he made me

believe it all mattered.

But I remember now.

I remember

the confusion,

the ache,

the silence after soft words.

The endless struggle to

sparkle in his skies.

The way I twisted myself

into something smaller

so he'd have room to stay.

No.

Not again.

I breathe.

I ground.

I count the months of silence.

I whisper the truth

like a prayer I carved into bone:

I choose peace

over pieces.

And I will again
tomorrow night
when the haunting returns.
I will never go back again.

Blue Shouldn't Hurt Like This

I wish his eyes weren't so blue.
Not because I loved them—
but because they drown me
like lies dressed in summer skies.

That blue—
it made everything feel endless.
Like depth. Like promise.
Like maybe I could fall
and finally be caught.
But I never was.
Just tumbled
into silence,
waiting for answers
that never came.

His eyes were blue,
but not warm, not safe.

Not water to drink from,
not sky to wish under—
just ice in a glass I kept refilling,
hoping it would melt into something real.

I wish they were muddy,
forgettable...
Not simply regrettable.
I wish they weren't the kind
songs get written about,
sparkling with promises
he never said aloud,
and certainly never meant.

Because now,
every time I see that shade—
on strangers,
on the sky,
worn myself—
I remember
how something beautiful
can still be the thing
that breaks you.
How his eyes were never magic,
only illusions.

Not Even in Sleep

If the ache returns,

let it know:

You survived it.

You outgrew it.

You don't go back.

Not even in sleep.

Red Flags

I live for the fantasy,

the firsts:

First glance.

First touch.

First kiss.

First 'you feel different.'

But when real feelings begin to bloom—

when he calls just to hear my voice,

when he wants to know what makes me... me—

I choke on the soil.

I uproot myself

before anything can take hold.

I say I hate red flags,

but maybe mine just look prettier—

maybe I've learned to color them

with good intentions

and poetry about self-awareness.

Maybe I pull away

because love feels like
standing on the edge of a cliff
with no wings,
just the memory
of how many times
I've already hit the rocks.
How many times
I've bandaged wounds
and covered scars.
So yes—
I say I want love.
But maybe
what I really want
is the idea of it.
The chase.
The ache.
The almost.
The parts that hurt less
when they fade away.
And maybe the biggest red flag
is hanging
from my own heart.

Weight

The mirror doesn't clap
when you jog for miles
without stopping.
When you pull a muscle
reaching for a milestone—
so far removed
from your original goal
of thinner thighs.

It doesn't cheer
when you choose water
over the things
you once reached for
just to fill the ache,
or when the protein bar
takes the place
of a stop at the drive-through.

It doesn't say,
"Look at you go,"
when you hit the 5K.
But you don't need that, anyway.

Because you know
what it means
to fight for progress
in a world that only rewards results.
To stand in front of your reflection—
sore, sweaty, not smaller yet—
but lighter in shame.

You know what it takes
to lace up your shoes
on a Tuesday night
when no one's watching.
When the scale is stuck.
When the air is thick.
When your legs are tired—
but your heart whispers,
"Still, we go."

Two and a half months.
Thirty-six pounds.

But it isn't just about weight.

It's about the late nights
you didn't let quitting win.
11:30 p.m.—tired,
but still putting down steps
on a seemingly endless belt.

It's hours spent in sneakers,
hoping it makes a difference.
Learning how to do it—
without overdoing it.
Old habits die hard.

It's the quiet hope
that maybe someday,
thin won't be as in—
and strength will start to sell.

It's every "maybe tomorrow"
that finally became today.

I don't need someone else
to be watching—

because for
the first time
in a long while,
I am all I need.

My reflection
is one of beauty—
whether
the mirror sees it
or not.

Before Flight

I broke open in silence.
No thunder,
no chorus of light—
just the sound of skin giving way
to something magic,
a new version of myself.

The dark did not let go easily.
What once was held on tightly,
with an iron grasp.
Even as I outgrew it.
Even as my back split
under the burden of becoming.

I did not emerge whole.
Just a different kind of heavy—
drenched in the past,
my wings trembling with stories.

Still wet with grief.
Still dripping regret like sweat.

But even that is part of the myth:
that flight begins with certainty.
It doesn't.
It begins with waiting and hoping,
as a branch creaks beneath you,
in a changing body you barely know,
beneath a sky you're not sure wants you.

You fear it won't hold you—
like so many others before.
But still, you wait
for the moment you are ready
to take flight.

I am not fearless.
I am not finished.
But I am no longer hidden.

And maybe
that is its own kind of miracle—
to rise slowly,
half-shadow,

half-light,
and trust these new wings
were made for sun and sky,
for comfort and flowers.

To believe they will know
how to open
when the moment is right.

;

Before the World Woke

When I arrived,
the bay held its breath.
Not a ripple stirred—
not from boat,
nor bird,
nor breeze.

It was mine,
just for a moment.
A world washed clean
by sleep and salt.

The lighthouse stood alone,
like me—
watching, remembering,
saying nothing.

I traced the edge of the tide,

barefoot,
brushing past yesterday's footprints,
picking up pieces
of the morning's offering.
But morning is a brief spell,
and peace never stays idle.

By late hour,
the stillness cracked
with ferry horns,
with jetskis and laughter,
with sandals kicking sand
as whole families arrived,
carrying coolers and towels
and stories of their own.

For a beat too long,
I resented them.

Their joy,
their noise,
their right to this beach
that, for a little while,
I'd called mine.

But then a family
asked me to take their photo
with the lighthouse behind them...
and I said yes.

Of course I did.
Because I have that photo, too.

With my parents,
when they were both alive.
With my children,
when they were still small enough
to climb into laps
without asking.

This place holds all of us.
Not just in silence,
but in snapshots.
In laughter.
In the way the tide
never stops returning.

Pretty Girl

Someone called me pretty girl today.
Only the second person in my life.
The first was you.
This time, it hit strangely...
not enough to split me open,
but enough to make my ribs remember.

The air caught between my teeth,
and my pulse stuttered
like I'd tripped over a ghost.
But I recovered quickly.
Faster than I thought I could.

It still hurt,
but it wasn't the same
nail-through-the-heart ache
I carried months ago.

Love (or whatever I mistook you for)
is restless, fickle,
afraid of its own shadow.
It faded into nothing,
leaving me to sweep up the glass.

Forcing me to rebuild myself
with hands that still shake,
thread that snaps,
and pieces that don't fit
the way they used to.

We grow stronger, yes...
but never unscathed.

Some scars sleep quiet,
buried deep.
That is until someone
leans in close,
mouth warm, voice low,
and says pretty girl...

And then, every scar I ever had
opens its eyes.

Blocked

At three a.m.,
the quiet is loud.
Fingers hover above the phone—
muscle memory searching
for a number that no longer exists
in my phone book.

I remember the first night
I pressed block.
How my chest ached
as if the word itself
were a locked door
slamming between you and me.

The first week,
I dreamed in conversations,
waking to nothing.
The first month,

I checked the blocked folder,
hoping the silence
wasn't as absolute as it seemed.

But it was.
Every time.

Not a single message,
not a single sign
that, even after everything,
I had been worth it.

The truth lands heavy:
I was never enough
for the person
who was never mine.

And tonight,
the phone rests face-down...
The ache is still there,
but so is the block.
I'll never reach out again.

The Folder

I loved him—
or maybe I didn't.
He was every red flag
I swore I'd never chase again—
casual, cold,
always halfway gone.
And still,
I wanted him.
Desperately.
It couldn't have been
just his eyes,
or the way night unraveled
between us,
skin and whispers tangled
until morning felt far away.
...No...
I think I loved
knowing I'd never have him.

That it was safe

because it was doomed

before it even began.

No need to write

an escape clause

when the ending

was already signed off on.

Still—

some nights,

I wish I'd find

a message in my blocked folder.

Just one line to prove

that what we had,

however small,

however doomed,

however insignificant overall,

was real to him too.

I don't know if it was love,

or just something shaped like it—

but months later,

it still hurts the same.

The Mask, Not the Man

I miss your eyes,

the way they burned through me,

the way they whispered promises

your mouth never spoke.

But they were the mask, not the man.

A flicker of light

on a hollow stage,

a performance so convincing

I almost believed.

I mistook hunger for devotion,

silence for depth,

the pull of your gaze

for the weight of your heart.

And still, I miss them.

Because even a mask

can feel like salvation

to someone aching to be seen.

But I see clearer now.

Eyes may glitter,
but they can lie.
And, the man behind them
never stayed long enough
to love me back.

Blooming in Silence

She was gone.

Again.

I knew it by the sobs

that drowned my voice

when it was too broken

to be born from my lips.

It was a dream, yes...

but when I woke

the tears still came,

the loss felt new.

A garden rose around us:

wild things for the pollinators,

roots remembering

what I could not say with words,

without falling into a despair

so deep, I'd drown

or fade away entirely.

My father's hands
offered seedlings,
his face the age it was
when I was still a child.
His eyes the color of the years
before age and grief.

I pointed to seed packets
he held up in silence,
choosing without words.
He obeyed,
pressing them under the soil—
burying beginnings, not ends.

Each seed split instantly:
green rising in memorial,
in remembrance, in love.
Flowers bursting upward
like fireworks from the earth.

The chorus of color
tore open the hush,
lending silent voices when

it hurt too much to speak.

No words. No sounds.
The pain had stolen them
from my throat, my heart.
Only silence flowering,
showing loss and beauty
growing from the same stem,
aching in the same bloom,
forever remembering.

Curtains

Once upon a time,
there was a girl who loved a boy.
But he didn't love her back.
Not in the way she ached for.

He kept her waiting
in the velvet folds of the curtains,
half in shadow, half in light,
with no promises,
and no release.

He said he owed her nothing.
After all, he'd made no promises,
never claimed her.
Hot, then cold.
Everything, then nothing.
Breadcrumbs scattered
just enough to keep her near.

He lived on the pedestal she built,
while she lived off of "maybe somedays."

He should have said the truth—
"I'm just not that into you,"
or, "It's time to let go."
But he didn't want to lose
the way she made him feel,
the access to her heart
he never intended to have,
to hold, or to keep.

It dragged on.
Years blurred into grief
until she learned to read
the words between his lines.
Until she saw the silence
for what it was:
a door he'd never open.

And still she misses him.
Sometimes.
Misses his eyes, his voice,
the way almost-love

once filled the emptiness.
But she knows the truth:
his affection was poison,
a sweetness laced with ash.

He was never hers,
and never would be.
And her heart deserved
something more
than breaking on repeat.

So she stepped out from
behind the curtains,
into her own light.
She left him behind.
Aching, but free.

About the Author

Regina Bergen lives with her children and rescue dogs in the beautiful Hudson Valley region of New York. She has a B.A. in Environmental Studies and Latin American Studies and a Master's in Public Administration.

Regina believes that genre boundaries are meant to be crossed and has published rom-coms, several volumes of poetry, a middle-grade fiction book about a rescue dog, and is currently trying her hand at a romantic fantasy retelling of the Garden of Eden story, *The Garden of the Fall*.

Before she began writing and editing full-time, she worked for many years as a fundraiser at a global environmental conservation organization, then spent several years as a stay-at-home mom. She loves the outdoors, animals, cooking, coffee, and spending her free time with her kids and pets.

Get in Touch & Other Books

Connect with Regina!

Social Media:
Facebook, TikTok, Instagram, Goodreads:
ReginaBergenAuthor
Substack: Regina Bergen Author
Website: www.ReginaBergen.com
Email: WritingbyRegina@gmail.com

Be sure to check out these other books by Regina:
Poetry: Amidst Fading Blooms; Secrets Unearthed, Petals Unfurled; and The Venom and The Rose
Rom-Com: *The Small Town Dirt Series*: Dirty Hoe – A Gardening Romance, Dirty Latte – A Coffee Shop Romance
Middle-Grade Fiction: Paisley, Untethered – A Rescue Dog's Tale

www.ingramcontent.com/pod-product-compliance
Lightning Source LLC
LaVergne TN
LVHW041226080426
835508LV00011B/1096